Vagabonding Guide
The Art of the Vagabond Travel - Satisfy your Wanderlust & Plan Long Term Travel on Budget

The little book for those who think they can't travel long-term but feel they want to

Table of Contents

Vagabonding Guide for First Time Travelers 1

The little book for those who think they can't travel long-term but feel they want to 1

Introduction 3

Chapter 1: Is Vagabonding For You? 6

Checkpoint #1 12

Chapter 2: The Downsides They Never Tell You About 14

Chapter 3: Preparing Yourself Mentally for the Big Trip 17

Chapter 4: Quitting Your Job 20

Checkpoint #2 22

Chapter 5: Funding, Funding, Funding 23

Chapter 6: Creating Fund Pools 29

Chapter 7: Transitioning to a Minimalist Lifestyle 34

Chapter 8: Plan Where You Want to Go 42

Chapter 9: It's Not a Vacation 49

Chapter 10: Vagabonding with a Companion and The Mistakes You Should Avoid 57

Conclusion: Adjusting to Life After Long Term Travel 60

Introduction

What is vagabonding? It is more than just another week long vacation. It is more than just a weekend getaway. It is actually a way of life. Best-selling author Rolf Potts describes it in such a simple yet powerful way as:

"A deliberate way of living that makes freedom to travel possible"

Vagabonding is a way of life. It's that simple. When you vagabond you choose your experiences. You also choose the type of adventures that you will have.

When you finally take the first step in that direction you can say it is your way to step out of the hamster wheel. You're walking away from the lifestyle of working hard day in and day out just to have small moments in your life to experience life in the real world.

You actually flip things around. You no longer work for material things. You travel and work (yes, there is still work—big grin) but you get the experience up front. In this book we'll go over the steps that I have learned from personal experience, which includes both the good and the bad actually, to live minimally and experience what life in the world is actually like.

Nope, It's Not a Vacation

Does vagabonding mean you will no longer see your friends and family anymore – of course not. You can still go back home and tell your friends and family about your adventures.

It's not a lifestyle that severs you from your roots. In fact, you may even help inspire others to break free of their mundane routines and perhaps tag along with you for a while. But that is not the goal of all of this and vagabonding is not for everyone.

In this book we will also give profile you if you are fit for this lifestyle or not.

Is there a difference between vagabonding and a month long vacation? They can surely sound very similar at times. Well, what's a vacation anyway? First off, the answer lies in how long a time you spend on vacations.

It's different every time, right? Some vacations last only during the weekend. There are vacations that last a week or maybe 10 days long. It sometimes depends on the vacation package that you signed up for.

Vacations are expensive—no doubt about that. It is relaxing and absolutely enjoyable. It's a healthy break from the crazy world at work. Sometimes you wish that your vacation can last forever.

But it can't, right?

You take pictures—lots of Instagrammable pictures that you can share with your friends but really it is also a way for you to remember what it was like to be there.

The worst part isn't the actual vacation but the aftermath of such a vacation. You will then try to catch up on work and life after vacation. Why, well because in our modern lifestyle the vacation is the illusion and work is life—the real life.

What if I tell you that there is a way to turn that around. Your vacations will become your real life and you make work the illusion. Catch that vision and you have learned half of what this book is all about.

Who then is the vagabond?

A vagabond today is one who never stops traveling. They may stop at certain points to earn money or maybe come home to catch up with loved ones. But they are always looking for their next stop along the road.

They don't put a lot of value on the next job they get even though it can be a high paying one. They don't earn money so they can buy the next stylish gadget. They're not in it for the lifestyle. They don't do it to impress other people.

They actually save money so they can go off again on their next adventure. That's the goal. They try to get back to life as soon as they can.

Vagabonding ultimately is retiring before you retire.

People work their whole lives and save up for retirement. But have you ever asked yourself why do you have to wait until you're old enough to retire? There is no guarantee that when you get old enough that you will be healthy enough to travel.

All of us spent our time to get rich enough so we can travel. Unfortunately the ironic part is that when we finally think we have enough wealth to cover for that expensive travel is that we have very little time left. In this book we'll cover how you can retire now before the day you actually retire.

Traveling is expensive and vagabonding is all about traveling.

Isn't vagabonding expensive? It may surprise you that it isn't as expensive as you think it is. The big question that is on people's minds when they hear about vagabonding and people who vagabond is how to finance all that traveling.

There are actually plenty of ways to cough up the cash needed to fund your travels. A huge portion of that comes from lifestyle changes that you can make on your own. In short, the way to do it is to live a minimalist lifestyle.

Sometimes all you need is to answer a few simple questions. First off, do you really need to buy a new car? Why buy a new car? Is your old car still working fine and dandy? If it is doing the job it's supposed to and it's doing it pretty well, then there is really no need to buy a new one.

You don't need 500 cable channels. You don't really need to get the latest pair of Nikes. You don't need to try the food in that new fancy restaurant that just opened over the weekend.

If you learn to prioritize your needs over your wants then you'll be surprised to find a lot of avenues where you can accumulate some cash to fund your next adventure. In this book we will go over that and other ways for you to fund your vagabonding trips.

That and all the other details will be covered as we go along into this new perspective in life.

Thanks for downloading this book.

Chapter 1: Is Vagabonding For You?

Vagabonding may seem like "the life" for many people. There may have been times when living that nomadic lifestyle has crossed your mind. Some people even dream of it and some would say it is their very own version of heaven.

However, I would just like to give you a heads up. Consider it as a bit of fair warning. Living the life of a vagabond—and this might demystify some people—is very much like living the same life you're life you're living in (you know the clock in-clock out 9 to 5 grind of life thing).

Vagabonding has its perks and it also has a lot of downsides. Sometimes it can be absolutely unrewarding and there were days when I wished I was home. It has its disadvantages and sometimes they can make you want to pack up and leave.

So Why Did I Keep At It?

I can compare the busy hectic chaotic and sometimes merciless corporate life and the simple life I live as a vagabond and I choose the less stressful and more rewarding simple vagabond life.

That's the reason.

The perks outweigh the cons and that is good enough for me. However, I will also be the first to admit that this lifestyle is not for everyone. It all depends on how you are hardwired and also I guess how willing you are to let go of the reality that you now live in.

In this chapter I'll spill the beans and tell you both the ups and downs of a vagabond lifestyle. Um, I'll emphasize the downsides more on this chapter to give you the real deal.

You may already have a good idea about the pros of vagabonding but you definitely need to know what you are about to give up and what quality of life you're about to plunge into.

It's fair. It's only fair to let you know what you're about to get before you jump right into this bandwagon. Of course you can always go back—no one's stopping you. And I'll give you a few tips that will help you along that will serve as your lifeline in case you figure out in the middle of your journey that vagabonding isn't for you.

It has happened more than once when a fellow journeyman that I have met has decided that he wanted to go back to the "civilized" (pun intended) life that he used to have. He missed his car and the great lifestyle that he had.

The good news is that he had things sorted out so that in case he went back he still had something that he could turn to. I had a few things in place myself but they were not as elaborate as his. Good for him.

So, I guess if that can happen to two or a few other vagabonds I met along the way, then that may happen to you to. Anyone is entitled to change their mind.

Are You Ready for This?

So, let's go over the details that you should know about vagabonding before you think of it as the ultimate vacation. Yep, that's what some people think vagabonding is all about. They think that it is nothing more than a long term vacation. You always have a piña colada in your hand, lying around in a hammock somewhere with beautiful beaches surrounding you.

Now, that right there is a vacation. That's not vagabonding.

If that is how you envision a vagabonding journey then stop. Just go on a vacation. It will do you much good than attempting to vagabond. A vacation is a better option for you if you have that kind of a mindset.

Here are some of the major aspects of vagabonding that they don't tell you on documentary TV:

- ***You Always Move Around***

A vagabond will always switch locations. You are on a constant move. Sure you can stay in a new town maybe to find work there to beef up your finances. However, the work you find there will always be temporary.

I a girl who used to be a superb accountant and she stopped by in St. George, Utah. She had a couple of relatives there and they needed an accountant to get their books sorted. She was there for about 8 months and was only there to save up money for her next stop—Amsterdam.

By the time I got there she almost had enough money and she was about to quit her accounting job. She was earning good money but since her priority was her travels then she didn't look at it as something for the long run.

You see, if you commit to a vagabond lifestyle you should view the changing environment that you're going through as your home. It's not that the road is home— you're not a homeless guy.

But your priority is not the job, not the place that you have discovered, but the new experiences and the changing environment. Those are your priorities. Oh you will need to go back to your comfort zone—it maybe the home where you grew up in when you were a kid or it can be in the presence of family and friends.

But you always move on to the next trip and to your next adventure.

- ### *The Vagabond Lifestyle is Above Everything Else*

Can you keep assets while you're living a vagabond life? Yes you can. You can keep some of your cash in a time deposit and leave it there for a year or more. You can let your relatives live in your house while you're away especially if they're out of luck and maybe struggling financially. It's a good way to help them out and it's the perfect win/win since you can also live the life you want as you do.

I also have a friend who switched from being a managing partner to financing partner (I don't know exactly what he was called) but he just let his other business partners manage the company and he just called in at least once a month and helped to make some of the business decisions from far away.

So, what's the point of all of this? All I am saying is that if you want to live this kind of lifestyle you should put vagabonding first above all else. You should be able to sacrifice anything so you can keep this lifestyle.

If your career is getting in the way then you can let go of it without any second thoughts. Religion, finances, career, and material possessions shouldn't get in the way of your choice to live the life of a vagabond.

Maybe that is why a lot of vagabonds I met on the road are actually Buddhists. It's a good fit, I think. Buddhism teaches its disciples to let go of things especially material possessions. A vagabond should be able to let go of their current state and hit a proverbial reset switch and start over in a new location and live a new adventure.

- ### *Zero Attachments*

Okay so we already established the point that you should put the vagabond lifestyle above all else. That also implies that you should break away from any attachments. Sure you will cherish the people that you get to know along the way.

You will make friends as you go and some of them are really good people. However you aren't supposed to make any attachments. What is an attachment? It is anything or even anyone that will keep you away from living the life of a vagabond.

Sure you will meet someone who will make you fall in love. Well, I have had a few in my time. But even though it hurt and it broke my heart several times I had to say goodbye and usually it was for good.

Remember—no attachments.

Most of these romantic interests that I met weren't willing to live a vagabond lifestyle and they were already comfortable with their lives the way things are. I had to respect that and if someone really loved me then they should respect my way of life as well.

- ### *You Always Pack Light*

Now, going along the lines of living life with no attachments, you should also commit to a minimalist lifestyle. I know I have mentioned that before in this guide several times now.

I think the Japanese folks have it right. You see I have gone around enough and I have met a good number of Japanese tourists. You know what is the one thing common about all of these people? They always travel light.

When they visit new locations they are there for the experience. Sure they may buy a souvenir or two but they're in it for the experience rather than the stuff that they can bring back home.

That means when they visit a new place they are in the moment every step of the way. The experience is the reward not the souvenir. And I think that is something that we all must learn—to relish the moment while we are there because that is where true value lies.

Souvenirs remind us of the experience but what is there to remember if you didn't take the time to bask in it in the first place. The things that you accumulate along the way will also become attachments that will eventually hold you back.

Imagine vagabonding for an entire year and you take lots of souvenirs with you each time you get to a new place. Imagine how heavy a load you will be carrying with you by the time you're done for that year. What are you going to do with all that stuff anyway?

That is why you should commit now to live a minimalist lifestyle. Don't buy stuff just to get stuff. Buy only the things that you need and prioritize the things that you need. If you buy a tool or pretty much anything, buy it and use it to the very last. If it still works then there really is no need to get a new one.

- *Live an Easy Life*

A vagabond is one who doesn't take life too seriously that it gets them depressed. It was about a year or so when the realization finally dawned on me. I was living in the third town and I was making friends with the locals.

I was having lunch with a new friend I made and I even bought him some nice fried chicken since they said it was the best recipe in town. I just had to check it out for myself. One of the goals I had with my vagabonding was to sample the best cuisines wherever I went.

The chicken was absolutely great. I even took pictures of the meal I ate before I took my first bite. My new friend, her name was Nancy, told me how she lost a friend the other day. They have been friends for many years and she said that she was going to miss her terribly.

That made me thought of home right then and there. I was having this delicious fried chicken and Nancy made me miss home. That wasn't the only thing I missed. I didn't realize how attached I was to all the people I met along the way.

I pulled out my phone—it wasn't an iPhone, it was this small old Samsung that I had for years. It still works so it's still the only phone I have. I kept all my pictures online so that I wouldn't have to worry about storage.

I checked out the pictures of all the people I have met along the way and showed them to my new friend Nancy who was already feeling sad – and she was also having some of that delicious fried chicken (damn you Nancy! That was good chicken—but we're still friends to this date).

It was then I realized that I had to live life easy. Each new move will mean that I will lose friends. But each new move also meant that I get to meet and make new ones.

Each new person, each new place, each new culture, each new experience adds to my soul. I understand people a lot better and I have become more accepting of others regardless of our differences in attitude, religion, point of views, political affiliation, and worldview.

I have learned to live and let live and be curious without being judgmental.

I honestly have learned about a lot of things from how to fix a car to designing a simple website from the folks I met along the way. I will sure miss a lot of them but I am happy to have met them.

- ***Take Things Slowly***

This is probably one of the biggest things that attracted me to the vagabond lifestyle. I know what it's like to live life in the corporate setting. Everything is fast, decisions are crucial, but you lose sight of the things in life that really matters.

I was stressed out and I needed to find a way out. Vagabonding was answer for me. Nowadays I usually take my time. Sure I take on jobs from time to time but I still take things slowly.

I usually stay in a new town or city for about a few months—I'd say three to four months on average. In some towns I stay longer and I had was in this one place where I stayed for a year.

I take my time and I get enough time to really get to know people. Small towns are great coz everyone knows everybody and I have learned to get that dynamic. I think that some of the most meaningful friendships I have made were made while I was vagabonding.

- ***Be Curious and Respectful***

In my travels I have learned to let a lot of things slide. Not everything will go your way and you can be sure as hell that not everything will go as you planned. So, don't over plan things and just go with the flow.

Be curious about a lot of things. Ask around. Learn from everyone you meet. Be respectful to everyone and I do mean everyone. There will be lots of people who will be mean to you.

That's normal—you're an outsider and most people aren't that quick to trust an outsider. We are social creatures so even though you are vagabonding you will have to meet and come to terms with everyone. And that includes the people who aren't hospitable and people who are also abusive.

The world is full of predators. You need to keep your wits about you when you're vagabonding. Being respectful also means you have to know your boundaries and keep yourself safe.

That also means you have to learn how to defend yourself at times. Research an area first, learn the local laws, and make sure to abide by all those laws while you're there so that if something goes wrong (and it has happened to me a few times) the locals have no reason to suspect you of anything.

Checkpoint #1

Pros and Cons of Vagabonding

Here are the ***pros of a nomadic vagabond lifestyle***:

- You have the freedom to go wherever you want
- You live completely independent of anyone because you are expected to be self-reliant
- There are always new places to see, new people to meet, new cultures to experience, and new things to learn about
- You become more aware of and more careful of the things in life
- You devote more time and attention to the things in life that really matter
- Improve your creativity and understanding through experience
- Travel can be cheap—you live by the cheapest living standards possible living like the locals
- You live a minimalistic lifestyle thus it is very easy to get organized
- You grow rapidly as a person and develop compassion and humanity rather quickly but understanding the best and worst in all people
- You become more outgoing and sociable since it is a necessary skill to survive out there in the world

Now Here are the Cons

- You miss out on a lot of important and often life changing events in the lives of friends and family
- Friends sometimes grow apart
- Fewer social support
- There's never enough storage space—you're always on the move so you should skimp out on souvenirs and memorabilia
- You can't host parties
- Potential employers will see a lot of black holes on your resume—and you have to explain that a lot times
- You have to deal with the bureaucracy like a rock stuck in your shoe while running a marathon
- Sometimes saving for future needs can be quite challenging
- It can be very exhausting since you move around a lot

- Things will be very difficult especially when you travel overseas if you don't have the necessary life skills
- Being a foreigner in a strange land can be a bit of a challenge to the psyche

Personal Checkpoint: Ask yourself if all of these things work well for you. Take the time to evaluate where you stand. Consider all the info provided here and in the previous chapter. Compare yourself to all of the points that have been raised both the good and the bad and then decide if all of that will fit your profile.

Chapter 2: The Downsides They Never Tell You About

The life of a vagabond isn't all fun and games. Sure you have left the world that is full stress behind but you still have to find a way to finance your needs from day to day. It's not a vacation rather it is a new way of life.

There is a reason why vagabonds are a minority in the world. As stated earlier, not everyone is fit for a transient lifestyle. Here are some of the reasons why people may not want to transition into or switch to this kind of lifestyle.

It's the Lonely Road

You will usually hear of stories of vagabonds talking about all the people they have met along the way. You will hear of peculiar folks with sometimes strange lifestyles. The further you travel away from home the more exotic the people seem to become.

However, what people don't always tell you is that a lot of times you will be traveling alone. It will not always be that easy to find a companion or at least someone who will be willing to talk to you.

You will almost always be surrounded by strangers—that is until you make them your new set of friends. If you are not the type of person who is comfortable living by yourself then this kind of lifestyle may not be for you.

Loneliness is a powerful and scorching feeling. Do vagabonds enjoy such feelings? Of course not—they're people too.

Are there ways to get over it? Of course there are. You can always call home and say hi to your loved ones every once in a while. You can contact them on social media and you can also update them on your blog. If you have friends and family who also blog about their lives then you can get updates there too.

Nevertheless, you will one day come to realize that living the life of a vagabond will entail a massive amount of loneliness. Loneliness will be your long-term companion. Oh yes, you will improve your social skills since you need it to survive on the road. You will learn to make friends quickly and that will be one of the tools you will use to get over being lonely.

Vanishing Private Space

You may be the guest in many places but remember that a lot of times privacy will be nonexistent. You will be a stranger in many lands and they will scrutinize you. Of course you will have your passport, IDs, and other documents. But that will not stop others from suspecting you of something.

You will learn quickly that in some places, trust isn't something that is given away freely. You have to prove that you are trustworthy. The way you behave in town during your first few days staying there will demonstrate to the authorities and the people in general who you truly are.

However, there will be times even after staying in a new place for months on end that you will learn it isn't quite like home. It may be your temporary home for the moment but it is never completely home. Well, that is until you make it so—that means finally deciding that you will settle in that new place for good.

Ups and Downs

Life goes on no matter you live the regular life or the vagabond life. While on the road you will learn rather quickly that there is really nothing regular or stable in life. You are constantly on the move and so is life—it will always be moving and things will always be changing even if you are some of the most idyllic parts of the world.

These changes will sometimes bring you to an emotional roller coaster. It's one of the challenges that you will have to contend with. If you let your emotions get the best of you then you will give up.

The Excitement Never Ends

When you're on the road you will find a lot of exciting experiences. Some of them might get too exciting even for the best of us. Have you ever seen a shootout between armed suspects and the police? Imagine getting caught in the middle of the fire fight. Worse, you can easily become one of the suspects since you're the stranger in town.

If you happen to travel to one of the snow-capped areas of the world, you will find yourself in one of the most unforgiving climates ever. Wherever you go there will be something that will be out of the ordinary and if you're not up for that sort of thing then vagabonding may turn out to be one of the things that you should avoid.

Financial Issues

Well, you don't have your regular job anymore, right? You no longer have that steady source of income. That means that even though you're on the road you should still find a way to earn something and make money.

Please excuse the shameless plugging, but that is also the reason why I wrote this and other books. Here I am writing about my tips and also my experiences on the road. May they help you realize what vagabonding is all about and maybe prepare you for it in case you decide one day to do it yourself.

But on the other hand, this is also my way to earn some money on the side. Do I expect to earn enough money to become a millionaire with this book? Of course not—I have to take the time to write all of this down, go over it several times to fact check and spell check and also grammar check the thing.

And then after it does get published I also have to spend some time night after night to market it. There will be no book signing events or meet the author events well because honestly I won't be able to tell you where on earth I will turn up next.

But I do hope that people will find my insights here valuable enough to want to read through it and maybe purchase the book and recommend it to others too.

Later in this book I will share to you some of the best ways to continue to fund your vagabonding.

Missing Out on Family and Stuff

Perhaps one of the biggest downsides for me is missing out on a lot of family matters. I never got to see my kids grow. My family practically grew older while I was away.

Sometimes it feels like I'm in the army and I'm always away on a foreign mission. Some of my friends back home already have kids. Some of them had kids and are now growing up.

I try to catch up as much as I can but sometimes you can't help but feel that life has gone by just fine without you. Sometimes that also brings a certain amount of sadness. But hey, I get to come home some time in a year and I try to catch up with everyone as much as I can when I do.

These are some of the biggest downsides of vagabonding well at least for me. Some of the guys who have also done it may also pull up a thing or two. Just remember that if you think that these sacrifices are just a bit too much for you then maybe you should think twice about vagabonding.

Chapter 3: Preparing Yourself Mentally for the Big Trip

You can't just take the plunge into a vagabond lifestyle. There are actually a lot of things that you need to prepare before you make that really huge commitment. Remember that vagabonding is traveling for a very long time.

Sure you can dip your toes in the proverbial waters from time to time just to see if you have what it takes. But you can't push the boundaries that far and think that you already have what it takes just like that.

Note that you will have to shed a lot of routines that you may have grown accustomed to. A change in lifestyle is always a life changing moment. Sometimes you have to do it in several levels.

Remember, what most people see is the seemingly glamorous life of a vagabond (or a pair of vagabonds—usually a husband and wife pair or any other couple for that matter) who have quit their jobs, sold their companies, invested in some kind of fund that sustains them financially, and then they tour the world.

Oh if only everyone can do that but even seasoned vagabonds don't have it that easy. I can say that such cases as the one described above is more of the exception than the rule. A lot of us have to plan things carefully especially our finances.

The Pre Vagabonding Checklist

Let's go over the things that you have to get sorted out BEFORE you actually go vagabonding and living that nomadic lifestyle that everyone talks about. One of the first things you have to do is to get mentally prepared for this exotic trip of a lifetime.

- ### *Why Do You Want to Go Vagabonding?*

What is it that prompted you to want that change? You have to ask yourself that. And you know what, you have to go for it seven levels deeper. In his best-selling book, Dean Graziosi talked about going through things seven levels deeper.

That is an important way to go about something that is about to change your life. It's a simple exercise that will aid you into self-discovery. So do you do it?

It's this simple. The first step is to ask yourself why you want to do something. Dig deep and search hard to find your reasons for wanting this change. Remember that vagabonding will change you for life. Its impact will be so huge that it will turn everything upside down.

So, let's say your answer is that you want to quit living the rat race as Robert Kyosaki once put it. The next thing you have to do is to ask yourself why again a total of seven times.

After you give an answer to the first why ask yourself why again. In this case ask yourself why you want to quit the rat race. Dig deep again and find out with deeper contemplation why you want to get out of the rat race.

And after you get an answer to that ask again why you want to do what you said you wanted. And so on. Asking deeper and deeper for every reason you give. Doing this will pry you open layer upon layer, reason after reason, until you come down to the most deep seated reason why you want to go vagabonding.

This exercise in itself is a journey into self-discovery. You must find the deepest rooted reason why you want to give up all the things you have now for something that you only think you might get.

- ### *Define Exactly What You Want to Do*

You should have a few things planned out about this long term trip but don't make things too complicated. You see even the best plans can get spoiled and you really can't plan for everything out there in the wild (pun intended).

First off, plan how you will finance your trip. Will you use stock market earnings? Are there any other investments that can stream cash to you while you're away? You can also work while you're on the road.

If you're an artist you can book gigs and if the laws in that place you're in allow it, you can perform on the street. If you are an English major or maybe a school teacher and you vagabond in a foreign country where people will like to learn about the English language then you can teach English as a Second Language.

TIP: *You should have planned at least one or two ways to source some form of income. How do you select a possible income stream? The short and sweet answer is to monetize your primary talents.*

Other than your finances you should also plan what you want to do in your travels. Are you going to document things? Will you be there to try the cuisine? Start small business there or start charities etc. Promote your martial art? Will your main focus be on the local culture? Or will you just be there to experience what is life like in that part of the world? You choose your purpose beforehand and that will guide you along the way.

- ### *Where Do You Want to Go?*

The next thing you want to identify is where you want to go. You can't just hit the road and go anywhere. Some think that it is all about going where the road takes you. Well, that is oh so romantic but in real life that will just get you nowhere.

You might end up just in the next town and spend a few months there and that might not be exactly the kind of vagabonding experience you intended in the first place.

Plan where you want to go so that you can plan the other details. If you want to go overseas to a foreign country then you can save up some cash. Choose which part of that country you will go to.

Research the locals, find out where you can stay, how much is the cost of living, figure out if you can live on the local diet or not, and just find out how you may fit in.

- ### *How Long Will You Be Away?*

Some people say that this is the easy part. Well, it may not be that easy for everyone. There are professors, academic scholars, and other professionals who go on sabbaticals. They go away sometimes on a fixed amount of time or they go away indefinitely.

However which way you want it will be okay. If it is your first time to go vagabonding I suggest that you try it for at least a year or two to help you get a feel for it. But if you feel like six months is already enough for you then it's absolutely fine.

Like I said earlier, vagabonding isn't for everyone. The important thing in this phase is to plan or at least decide how long you will be gone. It kind of gives you some kind of structure anyway.

Chapter 4: Quitting Your Job

Quit your job? Nobody told me that I had to quit my job.

If you love your job that much then maybe vagabonding isn't for you. But if you liked it and thought that maybe you want to experience some kind of change then maybe vagabonding is still not right for you.

If you hate your job that much then maybe vagabonding isn't right for you. A job change, or maybe a change in career paths could be the solution for you. But vagabonding may just be too extreme.

Keeping a Security Blanket

Now, here's an interesting lesson I have learned along the way. Quitting your job is a tricky thing. In my case it was easy coz I already gave my 20 years to that company and they have blessed me quite graciously.

However, my boss who is a senior manager was kind enough to put a proverbial foot through the door so to speak so that in case I wanted to come back some time in the future I could.

That was so generous of him. So I took him up on that offer.

I went on a sabbatical at first and it lasted a little over a year. And I did come back and after I came back to that crazy hectic world for another year, I finally called it quits. I quit my job and eventually went on vagabonding for real this time.

TIP: *Don't burn bridges when you quit your job. Always leave in good terms with your employers. You don't always know if the vagabonding hype will live up to your expectations. So, allow your boss to hold on to your job post and try the nomadic life for a few months. If it works out for you, then great; contact your employer and tell him you might not be coming back. If vagabonding didn't turn out as you hoped then it will be a great opportunity to have your job back waiting for you when you return to your old life.*

So, how do you quit your job?

Now, here's the thing. Don't do it over the water cooler. Your boss won't like it and it's not a respectful way to do it. Don't go AWOL either. You're going to break your employment contract. You may even lose your severance pay and other benefits that you could have gotten when you leave your job.

Follow the usual protocol for employees resigning from their jobs. Your boss will want to interview you – and he/she will. There will also be a point when they will try to talk you out of it.

At the very least they will think that it is just something that you need to get out of your system. They'll say it's just a thing or a bucket list item that you have to put a check mark on before you can go on with life as usual.

Well, maybe they're right. And maybe they are wrong. But who cares right?

You will only know which way it will go after you have tried vagabonding for a bit. That is how you can decide.

But remember, follow the protocol. Get the paper work done. Leave with the good graces of the company. Maybe they will take you back again in case you want to come back, which will be great too.

Checkpoint #2

Make up your mind.

At this point you have to determine the reasons why you want to go on a nomadic trip around the world. You have to weigh the pros and cons of undertaking such a trip. Why? Because it will change your life – it will turn things around.

It's going to be a drastic change.

Define the following:

- Why you want to go
- Where you want to go
- When do you want to go
- How you will finance your trip
- How long you will be gone
- How are you going to explain it all to your friends and family

And finally you should also figure out how and when you're going to let your boss know of your plans. We'll cover that in the next chapter. Remember that you should tell your boss only when you have everything setup.

I suggest that you let your boss know of your plan about a month or so (depending on the terms of your employment) before you finally go out into the world. Note that some employment contracts may require you to give at least a 30 day notice.

That would give your employer enough time to find someone to take your spot temporarily or permanently. Some employers will have grown fond of their employees that they may hold their employment positions open until their return; we'll cover more about that in the next chapter.

SublimeWare
Travel Electronic Accessories
"Charge Anywhere, any device!"

Search all products... 🔍   🛒 CART

ABOUT US   OUR PRODUCTS ˅   NEWS   CONTACT US   SUPPORT ˅   WHOLESALE & CUSTOMIZATION

 5 USB Ports 🔌 WITH ONE TYLE C   🌐 Multi Country Adapter 150+ countries 5600MA / 5Vdc 8A. 110-230Vac

 Type-C

2.4A

 TYPE G
UK/HK/SINGAPORE

 TYPE I
AUST/CHINA

 TYPE A
US/CAN/JAPAN

 TYPE C
EUROPE/SOUTH AMERICA

Chapter 5: Funding, Funding, Funding

Traveling whether it is a weekend getaway or a 5 year sabbatical is expensive. That shouldn't be a shock to anyone. In this chapter we'll go over how you are going to fund that long-term travel that you have been planning for.

Funding your travels is one of the first things that come to mind whenever I bring up the subject of vagabonding to anyone. And I do mean anyone—whether I'm talking to a complete stranger on the road or whenever I talk to my folks at home.

Everyone asks—how can you afford all of that?

Some people are absolutely amazed at how I am able to do it. Here's a secret: choose your destination and you will be able to afford it. You will be surprised as to how cheap it is to live in other countries.

In one trip I had a friend with me and our combined budget was $40,000 and we planned to travel to Southeast Asia. We planned to stay there for about 15 months or so and then come back home to the US.

Believe it or not, that $40,000 was more than enough. In fact we were living a luxurious life.

However, one of the important things I learned is this, sure you have money saved up and that may be quite a lot in some parts of the world, and you have things planned so you're all good, right?

I learned that you should also still plan on having one or two income streams while you're traveling. You can also try working for local companies although jobs won't always be available. Working odd jobs for the locals can help you get immersed in the country's culture. But mind you the pay isn't that much.

Everything is so unpredictable out there. Traveling is unpredictable and so are the expenses. Is red tape rampant? Well it happens from time to time. Sometimes you have to grease the manager, some local authority, or an employee.

Now, here's the thing—avoid the under the table money. But you should quickly pickup on cultural norms. Sometimes you have to give away a dollar or two just to please the locals but there are times when your business is all that is necessary.

Sure some days are cheap but there are days when people look at you like you're some sort of money churning lucky charm. No matter how carefully you plan things there are things that pop up along the way that drain your funds.

Getting Started—Settle All Your Debts First

You can't travel and still worry about your student loan. You can't go on a wild adventure while worrying about your credit card bills that will be due in a couple of weeks. You won't enjoy your trip—obviously.

The first step to any form of freedom on the road living the nomadic life of a vagabond is to be financially worry-free. And that means you shouldn't have any debts left that need paying.

BIG TIP: *Don't quit your day job just yet.*

You're going to need your job to save money for your trip and you're going to need your job to pay for all the loans and debts. You need to get everything cleared out first.

That also means getting rid of your excess credit cards. You can keep one or two—at least that is my personal take on it. I have two credit cards still under my name but I don't use them as much as I used to. I only use them when I really run out of cash on hand.

Finding Work on the Road

A lot of people think that you can just live off any odd jobs that you can find while vagabonding. I wish that were the most readily available form of work when you're on the road.

Here are two reasons why this idea is just going to give you some trouble along the way:

1. There aren't enough odd jobs out there
2. The business owners will probably trust locals more than they would trust a nomadic stranger

Oh, I guess we can also squeeze a third one: the pay isn't always enough to fund your trip. Well, maybe it would be enough to get you food and pay the room you're renting. But you won't have enough moolah to fund your travel expenses to get you to your next stop on your vagabonding trip.

In my case you can say that I was fortunate enough to find freelancing gigs to keep the funds coming. I have a knack for writing—well, I write business proposals, copy, company newsletters, training materials, and whatnot. It was part of my job description.

If you want a more passive kind of income then try affiliate marketing. But mind you it will take time to build a reputation both via SEO and also through social media. Apart from that you will have to churn out a lot of work. I have seen only about 5% to 10%

success rate from my affiliate marketing efforts. The winning projects tend to pay for every losing project I come up with.

And so I monetized my innate talents.

It's hard to find clients on telecommuting sites like Upwork and others but I was able to establish myself as a credible worker even before I quit my job. Doing that at least gave me some form of side income even though I didn't get paid as much as what I get from my day job.

When I was on the road I had my laptop with me. There are plenty of pubs, cafes, libraries, B&Bs, and other places that had free internet. I also had my phone with me and sometimes I was able to use that as my portable hotspot. It depends on whether there was a carrier signal or not.

Speaking of the internet—if you plan to travel overseas then don't expect the internet in other countries to be as good as the ones you got back home. They usually suck—well, maybe except in Japan and Korea. However, if you're in places like Thailand, the Philippines, Vietnam, or other developing countries expect the internet to be a tad slower. In some areas it is turtle level slow.

That is why I stick to cafes and other places because they usually have faster than average internet than the ones offered by regular local telecom companies. I guess the regular consumer account has poorer quality compared to business accounts. Oh, if you find a Starbucks wherever you're going, then you're in heaven—they usually have better internet there. But the coffee is just as expensive.

So, other than telecommuting or working as a freelancer online, what are the other options to get some funds going your way? Here are a few suggestions I have in mind:

- *Find a temp or part time job while on the road*

Sometimes you may just need a short job that maybe lasts for 4 weeks just to get you right back on track. There are part time jobs that you can get like maybe at a diner, a store, and elsewhere that doesn't require a lot of skills.

Note however that you shouldn't expect these odd jobs to be around wherever you go. It won't be a regular thing and there will be plenty of places where there are no odd jobs since the people there don't need help doing stuff.

Sometimes your pro skills are necessary maybe as a handyman, carpenter, mechanic, bookkeeper, dressmaker, computer repair guy, electrician, etc. Sometimes there are online jobs that may require your clerical skills like typing jobs, working on Excel balance sheets, graphics design, transcription, website design, etc.

- *Do freelance work and build your clientele while at home*

If you have a knack for Photoshop, you're good at crunching numbers on a spreadsheet, you're a voice talent, you can write emails and interoffice correspondence, you take good pictures, etc. then you can do some freelance work and build your clientele even before you leave for your vagabonding trip. You can then go back to your freelance gigs from time to time even while you're on your trip.

- ### *Sell your photos*

What sort of photos can you sell? Well, pretty much anything. You can take pictures of people working, people hanging around, people at church, those who are in the office, and even in a diner. Just remember that in some photo sites, you may be required to submit a consent form if you take pictures of people.

You can also take pictures of cities and towns that you have been too. Take pictures of buildings, roadways, streets, bridges, the skyline, and anything and everything that you see around you.

You can of course sell pictures of food! You can even take pictures of empty plates, tables where food is served, what it looks like in certain restaurants, pictures of food from different cuisines, and others.

You can of course take pictures of mother nature. Sunsets are popular so there will be plenty of those. But you can also take pictures of the surrounding mountains, rivers, plains, trees and shrubbery, the nearby woods, grasslands, animals grazing or hunting, other people's pets, the beach, clouds, sand, rocks, and anything that Mother Nature can give you.

You can sell your photos in many sites and platforms. A lot of these are stock photo websites like the following:

- Adobe Stock
- Shutterstock
- Alamy
- Etsy
- Fotomo
- Crestock
- 500px
- Snapped4u
- PhotoShelter
- BlueMelon
- TourPhotos
- Displate

Another place where you can stock up on your photos and sell them online is through your very own website. You can create your own gallery website using WordPress and you can take advantage of the many plugins that you can use to design your photography site.

Are there advantages to selling your pictures on your own website? Yep, there are. Here are a few good reasons:

1. *You command the price of each photo* – note that in photo selling sites or stock photography sites, it's the site owner who dictates how much your photos are worth. They also get a cut from each sale you make. Sometimes your photo prices get jacked up but you don't get the entire amount described on the site.
2. *The payment is 100% yours* – no one gets a cut out of the work you put in.
3. *You have full control* – you control the price, you control the amount of photos being displayed, you control which of your photos get shown first to customers.
4. *Your website, your rules* – you don't have to walk the proverbial tightrope so to speak. There are stock photography sites where you can lose potential earnings simply because you broke a certain rule or something like that.
5. *You get to interact with customers directly* – customers can contact you if they like what they see on your site. They may even commission you to take pictures of the things that you see in your travels. That way you get paid directly for pictures that your client wants. In effect you're traveling around taking pictures and getting paid to do it.

Create Apps

Do you have a knack for programming or designing apps? You don't even have to be a programmer. All you need is an idea for an app and then you can hire a freelance app developer and have him design it for you. You can then pay the guy and sell the app.

Find Work Overseas

You can find a job overseas. Some have taken the opportunity to teach English or some other subject that they are proficient in. Others offer consulting services. That is a great way to get into another country and experience the local life there. Of course you can schedule some time to travel outside of work as well.

Rent Out Your Home

If you plan to be gone for years on end then it would be a good idea to setup your home to be rented out. That way you can arrange for the money to get paid directly to your bank, which means you get some steady cash while you're away. You can hire someone to manage the place while you're away too.

Chapter 6: Creating Fund Pools

So now you still have your day job, you're now starting a side job, and maybe planning for your trip. The next big step is to create 2 fund pools that you can draw from. Yes, you will need 2.

1. Emergency fund
2. Travel fund

#1—Emergency Fund

Your emergency fund is the fund that you don't ever-ever-and I do mean ever touch until you really need it. It should be money that you can access anywhere and anytime. You can keep it on an online account or maybe in an ATM that you keep somewhere on your person always.

How big should your emergency fund be? Well, it's up to you. Here's the thing. Maybe here at home you are just getting by with $25,000 to $30,000 but if you go elsewhere like Asia or in South America you will be living the good life.

Well, at least you will be above the average Jose out there. You will have enough to pay for pretty much everything from food, housing, transport, clothes, and everything. Your 30 thousand will be worth several hundred thousand elsewhere.

So, how much should your emergency fund be? My best guess is about half of that. That way when things go south, and I do mean the deep south of it all, you have cash that you can pull out to get you home safely and comfortably.

TIP: *Don't live like a king when you're out there. Live frugally. In fact you should experience the local culture and live like the locals do. Eat what they eat, have fun where they have fun, splurge a little on some nights, ride the public transport, rent a cheap car if you must on certain days, and enjoy the company of the local folks. That way your $30,000 will sustain you for several months which should be enough to help you bask in the vagabonding experience.*

#2—Travel Fund

How much should your travel fund be? Well, we already mentioned that $25,000 to $30,000 is enough to help you live well in other parts of the world. That can be a realistic goal for now.

However, if you can manage to top that then that will already be quite an achievement. Let that amount be the first amount that will gauge if you are ready to be a vagabond. That will be your first challenge—raise your travel fund.

Again, this is money that you will never ever touch—well at least until you're on day 1 of your vagabonding adventure. This is an important rule and it is a powerful test of your commitment to go on a long-term nomadic travel.

It's a challenge because the world economy is changing. What was once called "financial security" by baby boomers and the gen-x crowd is slowly becoming something that is not totally feasible.

Currencies can topple down rendering funds you have saved as something of lesser value. The way people make money is changing fast. Technology is driving that change. And sometimes you just have to beat the current inflation rate just to make sure your funds stay afloat.

That is why saving up for your travel fund is the big test for you. If you can pull that off then there is a good chance that you have developed the discipline and frugality to live outside of your comfort zone and prepare you for life on the road.

Get Financial Advice—Never Leave Home Without One

If only people can become millionaires on their own then everyone should have been millionaires right? The fact is that most of the time, we all need financial advice to help us manage our money.

That is why I recommend that you get in touch with the cheapest financial manager that you know. It could be a friend who is doing well in life who can give you a few tips so you can raise the money for your long term travel.

He or she can help you find areas where you are leaking funds. For instance, do you have a Starbucks habit? You can say that $3 bucks a day spent on quality coffee isn't that much but when you sum it all up that would equate to $90 a month. That will equate to more than a thousand dollars a year if you just do the math.

Your financial adviser can give you more tips to help you build your nest egg a lot faster, which may include any of the following:

- Sell your excess goods (i.e. the stuff you accumulated and bought and never really got to use)—others refer to this as junk but another man's garbage is another man's treasure. Some people have made a good amount of money selling unused goods on eBay.

- Quit your gym membership
- Stop eating out—learn to cook your own food
- Sell your car and get a bike. But if you need your car then sell it and then get a less expensive one. You can even save up on car insurance if you downgrade your car.
- Quit your online viewing subscriptions
- Stop watching cable
- Downsize your house—you may be paying too much on mortgage

Your financial adviser can help you find all these loopholes and help you focus on your needs rather than your wants.

#3—Investments—Your Third Fund Pool

The rule of thumb here is not to put all your eggs in a single basket so to speak. You should start today and find other income streams. Your day job is already one, you may already have a second job as additional income, and then what is next?

Here are a few ideas:

- ### *Rent Out Your Home (or some other property)*

Do you live in an area where people will want to rent out homes? Will a little fixing maybe you can get your home prepped for rental. Do the math. If you rent out your home for the current rates in your area and you live in a dorm or a cheap apartment somewhere, will the rent on your home be enough to cover your rent and then some? If that is the case then renting out your home at the current or maybe higher than the current rate can be a good idea for another income stream.

- ### *Time Savings Account or Certificates of Deposits*

You can talk to your bank and setup a time deposit savings or a long term savings account or what is known as Certificates of Deposits (CD). This will be money that you can turn to after your travels are done. You come home, your travel money has been augmented (you will still work while on the road) and spent by the end of your trip, and you come home broke.

Well, not necessarily. If you have your emergency fund then you have some cash to turn to. And if you have time savings then you have some cash that has been sitting in the bank and earning some interest.

A CD simply put is money you loan to a bank so they can invest it in something else. There is a term length that lasts anywhere from 3 months to 5 years. During such time you will not be allowed to withdraw the money you deposited (i.e. loaned to the bank)—well there are ways for you to withdraw it but you will incur some costs.

Your money will then earn interest during the time it remains with the bank. This investment will grow at a fixed rate.

- **Bonds**

Bonds are pretty much like certificates of deposit and they function like so. In the case of bonds you are lending or loaning money to the government and in some instances to certain private corporations.

This type of investment is characteristically stable because you know exactly how much you're going to get back after your investment term is over. There is also a guaranteed return.

You can choose how long will the term of your bond will be. The terms include one year up to five years and even longer. Note however that the returns are smaller when you invest in bonds compared to other investments.

If you're the type that prefers to know exactly how much money you can get in the end then a bond is a good option for you.

- **Mutual Fund**

A mutual fund is one way you can invest in the stock market minus the technical know-how needed to select the right stocks to invest in. Picking individual stocks to invest on can be quite a daunting task and if you're on the road vagabonding you won't have time to keep an eye on different stocks so you can decide when to buy them and when to sell them.

You can join a mutual fund and your investment will be pooled with the money brought in by other investors. That pooled fund will be used by a fund manager—usually someone who is a seasoned veteran in stock market trade and investment.

All you have to do is provide the money along with other investors like you and the fund manager will use his expertise and earn you (and himself along the way) some profits.

- **Real Estate Investment Trusts or REITs**

REITs function like mutual funds but instead of investing the pooled funds in the stock market they will be invested in real estate properties. There will also be a manager who will manage the properties as well as the funds that have been pooled. The trust manager will also be a seasoned veteran in the real estate industry and will make a profit from the REIT if you make a profit.

Note that REITs can also be invested in other industries not just in the real estate sector alone. Some REITs can be invested in the construction of buildings, apartments, and other forms of infrastructure. They can also be used to construct healthcare facilities—that means there are some crossovers into other industries as well.

There are other industries where you can invest too. Some are of course a lot riskier than others. Examples of such investments include dividend yielding stocks and peer-to-peer lending or crowdlending.

Chapter 7: Transitioning to a Minimalist Lifestyle

When you're on the road there is no space for you to store the usual clutter. You will need to be more frugal and manage your finances even better. Remember that you don't have the security of a regular paycheck on the road.

And that is why transitioning to a minimalist lifestyle will help you prepare for vagabonding. This kind of lifestyle will create more time on your schedule, get you more money in your bank account, and you will get in touch with the more meaningful things in life.

So, what are the benefits of living a minimalist lifestyle? Here is a short list:

- *You create room for what is truly important*: the very first thing that you do when you decide to live a minimalist lifestyle is to purge your drawers and cabinets. Yes, it's almost like the Purge movie series—I know it's a bad pun but I'll use it anyway.

  You lose the claustrophobia of a cluttered home and you breathe in a new sense of freedom. You immediately see that you actually have a lot of space. You can also say that this is some sort of a ritual where you release yourself from all the fluff and create more room for the truly meaningful stuff to fill your life figuratively or otherwise.

- *It gives you more freedom:* this may not be apparent at first since it would seem that someone or something is making you get rid of your stuff. It would sometimes feel like there is someone who is forcing you or is control of you.

  However, once you get over the proverbial initial speed bumps that come along your way when you attempt to create a lifestyle change, everything clears up. One of the first paradigm shifts that happen is that you suddenly realize that the accumulation of material things is something akin to an anchor.

  An anchor is something that holds us in place—something that ties us down. Having that urge to get more things is like trying to make a car move forward with your foot on the brakes.

  We all have this native fear of losing our stuff. However, once you have tried letting go at least in the small ways at first, you will realize a new kind of freedom.

You will later realize that what you are really letting go of are not only your material possessions but the things that contribute to their accumulation which includes obsession, debt, overworking, and greed.

- **It allows you to focus on your hobbies and also on your health**: Don't expect to be able to go vagabonding if you have health issues. Don't even attempt it. Why? Health care services will not always be as good out there than it is at home.

  If you have health issues you should first check with your doctor if you're okay to travel. Take enough prescription medication that can last you your entire trip—or more if you can manage that.

  However, once you make the transition to a minimalist lifestyle you can have more time and resources to focus on your health and also your hobbies. You will find yourself spending less time in Home Depot and more time for yourself doing the things that you have always wanted to do—you know the things you usually thought you never had time for.

  People usually say that they don't have enough time but have you really taken the time to stop and evaluate the activities that take a lot of your time? Some of the activities you may be doing during your day may be taking you away from the things that really matter.

  Living this kind of lifestyle will free up chunks of your time so you can spend it on things that you love doing. It allows you to spend time with your family, workout and get some exercise, read the books that you love, do yoga (or some other thing that you have always wanted to do—it was yoga in my case), and of course traveling.

- **You tend to focus less on material possessions**: I have come to realize something along the way when I was learning to live a minimalist lifestyle. During that transition I had a huge paradigm shift when I started to realize that the stuff I accumulated filled my life with nothing more than distractions.

  Money can't buy lasting happiness. Nevertheless it can make life comfortable, correct? I have come to understand that after money and our possessions have done their part that should be the end of our obsession with it.

  However, that is not what popular media is flaunting nowadays. A lot of times you are told through many ads that happiness is measured through the canon of materialism. We try to resist the urge but the continuous messages we get bombard our senses with the suggestion and enticement that to have more is the path towards happiness.

I call that the consumer's trap. They lure us in through advertisements and then they keep you in there through a never ending cycle of things you never thought you need but you never really needed in the first place.

Take your focus off of those things and you realize that lasting happiness is not to be had through them. These are things you realize when you reach the twilight years of your life—when you have only so much time in your hands left to spend. Practicing minimalism brings you closer to that mindset and gives you more time because you realize these things now.

- **Peace of mind**: I have found that when we cling to material possessions we tend to become more stressed because we always have that fear of losing them. If the core of our focus is on money then wave that lingering fear that one day we may run out of money.

When we simplify our lives by living a minimalist lifestyle we lose that attachment to these material objects, which in turn creates a calmness that we may have forgotten. It is this calm peace of mind that we once had when we were younger. The fewer things you worry about the more peace you get in life.

We come to a realization that money can be earned and material possessions and all things temporal can be reacquired.

- **You will not have to fear failure that much**: Am I afraid to fail—of course I am. But I am not that afraid of it as I was before I became a minimalist. I have also observed that people tend to excel more when they are shown the limitless possibilities that are before them.

Sure they will experience failure one time or another but since they can see a clear vision of the opportunities ahead of them then they strive more in spite of their failures. Once you become a minimalist the fear of failure is no longer as significant when compared to the possibilities that life now offers you.

Sure you still need to work hard to put a roof over your head and get food on your plate. But you won't fear that as much because you know you have plenty of sources and plenty of options. You can always find a way to provide.

- ***You will find greater confidence***: Transitioning to a minimalist lifestyle promotes self-reliance and individuality. These are at the core of this kind of way of living. Being self-reliant is a great way to boost your self-confidence. The more you realize that you can better provide for yourself the better will your chances be when you finally go vagabonding.

Some people think that they need to be rich in order to travel the world. In my experience, the day I switched to a minimalist lifestyle allowed me to save more money. I have since quit my job and traveled to almost a dozen countries around the world.

So, how did I begin? Here's how.

Start Decluttering

I am what you can call the classic hoarder. I used to love—no wait—the right word is adore; I used to adore Ikea magazines, endless catalogs, and a lot of brochures. There were nights when all I ever did was to look at home TV shopping channels to look for the latest furniture fad.

Well, it doesn't have to be furniture. If it was some latest kitchen device, juicer, coffee pot, or whatever that looked great on my countertop, I just had to have it. That habit also meant more items that I had to pay for when the credit card bill came along.

Somewhere along the road I was bouncing my debts from one credit card to another. I was struggling hard to catch up. That went on for a while with me always hoping that I would be able to pay for everything.

Except that I always ended up buying new stuff so my credit card bills never really went away. Sure I paid off my old debts but then I had new ones coming along. It was a horrible cycle.

It took a good friend to help me out of that. She was kind enough to give me advice—financial advice and I guess that sparked the whole minimalist lifestyle episode in me. And one of the first things I ever did to get me started is to declutter my surroundings.

That meant I had to do garage sales every week.

And guess what. I accumulated so much stuff that when I finally sold everything off, I had more than enough to pay the last of my credit card bills with a little bit of savings on the side.

Was it easy?

No it wasn't. There was always that urge to fill empty spaces. And at times I clung to the things I bought so much that I thought I couldn't possibly sell them to anyone. My friend helped me decide. The first things to go were stuff I had never used for quite a while.

That went on and on—evaluating and admitting to myself that I didn't really use those juicers anyway. I had everything from Jamba Juice, Philips, Omega, Breville, and others. I had masticating juicers, cold press juicers, and centrifugal juicers. And those were just the juicers—don't get me started with the coffeemakers.

You can do that right now.

Go over all your stuff. Make a list of the *things that you actually use every day*. You'll be surprised that you actually only need a few things. We only use a certain minimal amount of items.

If you want to live a minimalist lifestyle start decluttering and live with that minimal amount of stuff that you use every day.

Start a Savings Account

Maybe you already have one and you just weren't paying attention to it. In chapter 6 we talked about making fund pools. Best practice dictates that we should create separate accounts for each fund pool.

If you don't have a savings account start one as soon as possible. The sooner you get that started the sooner you can get ready for your vagabonding trip. It will teach you to be frugal. It will teach you to manage your money wisely. It will also teach you to be more self-reliant.

Your savings will be your little nest egg that will help you to finally quit your day job and begin your transition to a vagabond lifestyle.

Now here's a tip: setup automatic transfers from your regular bank account to your savings account. You decide how much you want to put in there but if you really want to get it done real quick I suggest you set 10% of your pay each payday to be automatically transferred to your savings account. That way you don't have to think about it.

You can also set things up so that you can have a certain amount of money automatically transferred to your savings account. Well, that is if you think that 10% of your regular income is still a bit way too much. I have a friend that who started things off by automatically transferring $100 to her savings account each week. She was thrilled the day she found that she had $1,000 in her savings account.

Let it be a habit.

To speed things up I would advise you to cut back on your unnecessary expenses. Do you have magazine subscriptions, cable TV, Netflix, extra minutes and other features on your cellular phone plan, and other subscriptions that you don't really use? It's time to cancel those subscriptions.

After living a minimalist lifestyle for a while I was able to automatically transfer 40% of my regular paycheck to my savings automatically. Now, even if I wasn't planning for a long term trip I eventually had enough money in my savings I never knew I could come up with. Achievement unlocked!

Write Down Your Goal

Studies show that when people write down their goals that there is an improved chance that they will achieve it. Now, to make the chances go up you should write down that goal and post it in places where you can see it.

You can write it down on a piece of paper and stick it on your fridge door. In my case I made it the wallpaper on my laptop and on my phone.

I even had small sticky notes on my work desk. What was written on my goal? It was this:

"Travel = $40,000"

"Current total: xxxx"

The current total was the amount I had in my savings. Well, eventually I was able to make fund pools and had money set aside for emergencies, for travel, and other funds as well.

But the point is that the reminders and the fact that I see my goal every day helped me to stick to my commitments to live a minimalist lifestyle.

Learn to Shop Only for the Essentials

This was the hard part for me from the beginning. Well, minimalism doesn't mean you will live in a tent in some crazy neck of the woods. That's not even what vagabonding is all about. It's not like you're on Survivor or some reality TV show where they leave you to fend for yourself in a remote island.

You will still live life as usual but only without the excess of consumerism. You will still get food for your family. You will still buy your dog his treats. You will still get new clothes. You will still get the rest of the stuff that you need.

And that is the key right there—get only the stuff that you need.

You will have to learn to distinguish between your needs and your wants.

Now, having a savings account helped me. But the big thing that really helped get over the urge to splurge when I learned to create a budget and stick with it.

Before you take your money out shopping you should write down a budget. Here are a few simple steps:

1. Find out how much money you have right now.
2. List down how much of your pay went to your savings. Remember that this should be automatic.
3. Make a list of the things that you need. Make sure that they are essentials. This was the hard part for me—honest. You really have to make up your mind that this thing in your list is an essential.
4. Always have a shopping list and stick to buying only the items on that list.
5. No window shopping when you're out shopping. Stop looking at the things that had the "SALE" sign on it.
6. Get out of the store as soon as you can. The longer you linger the sooner the store gets you.

Plan 2 to 4 Weekend Getaways and Pack Light

This helps you to practice. I used to travel with a lot of stuff. You don't have to travel far. You can plan an overnight stay at the beach and stay in a cheap motel. The goal is to practice traveling and to learn how to pack light. This is something I learned from a Japanese friend.

Those guys always travel light. I learned that I can pack half the clothes I usually bring with me. I also learned that even some of the essentials (like toothbrush, soap, toothe paste, shampoo, drinks, snacks, food, sunscreen, etc.) can be bought on site. That means you don't really have to bring a lot of stuff when you travel.

Big Tip: Here's a radical way to get you jump started with packing light. We all have match luggage right? They can come with one really big luggage bag and it will come with a matching small one. Well, some Samsonite luggage bags are three piece sets—it depends on what you have.

Here's the big idea—use the smaller luggage bag when you go on your weekend trip. Try to fit all the stuff you need for your trip (just the stuff you need, mind) in that small bag. Don't bring anything else, just the stuff in that smaller bag.

That's the challenge.

Reduce Time Spent on Social Media

Social media can be a powerful tool for business and communication but for many of us regular folks we use it to check out our friends. It eats up a lot of our time—well that was my case.

When I decided to cut back on social media I was able to find more time to do more meaningful things. I was able to take walks in the park and appreciate Mother Nature. I was also able to visit with friends – like being there for them. Sometimes we need to disconnect more to reconnect with the important people in our lives.

Digitize Everything

Magazines, books, old photographs, and other bits of paper take up a lot of space. Convert them into digital format. You will also do the earth a favor.

Learn to Borrow Stuff You Don't Really Need to Buy

Minimalists tend to just borrow things that they don't use every day. This is a skill that comes in handy when you're on the road. You will have to use some socialization, friendshipping, and neighborly skills to do this. Of course, make sure to take care of the items your borrowed and return them promptly.

Get Rid of Something Before You Get Something

This is considered as a minimalist rule of thumb. Let's say you need a new pair of shoes. Before you buy a new pair, plan on how you will get rid of your old one—throw it in the trash give it away to someone who may need it (you won't believe that there are people in some parts of the world who can't afford to buy shoes). Once you buy the new pair, get rid of the old pair.

Eat Healthy yet Simple Foods

Learn to cook your own meals. This skill will be an essential to vagabonding. But you should learn to prepare and eat simple healthy meals. This habit helps you avoid fast food.

Learn to Appreciate the Little Things

As you make the move to a minimalist lifestyle you are preparing yourself for life on the road. One of the changes that you will notice about yourself is that you will learn to appreciate all the little things in life like the blessing of waking up to a new day, beautiful sunset, time spent with friends, and opportunities to experience life.

Chapter 8: Plan Where You Want to Go

Someone once asked the legendary Rolf Potts, yes that Rolf Potts who started this wave of vagabonding and nomadic lifestyle in our day and age, well someone asked him where should a first time vagabond slash digital nomad should go? Which would be the best places to start for a first timer?

What he said there were actually gems. He mentioned some of the best places in the world to start roaming around for any long term travel. He also emphasized that you don't have to have tons of money to do it. That means if you were able to able to create a sizable travel fund you don't have to spend it all on your first trip.

Potts recommended that for your first journey you might just want to road trip to places close to home. That is why I recommended that you should first do some test runs—aka weekend trips. He also recommended going to national parks, which is also a great idea. Well, I wasn't the outdoors kind of person back then so camping out didn't appeal that much to me.

But what if we want to go on that BIG journey? Which places should one try first? Well, here are his recommendations:

1. Europe

For some of us Europe is truly a dream travel destination. You might want to try Amsterdam, France, London, Italy, Prague, or any of those big name places. The downside of course is that these places are usually some of the most expensive places in the world. I would say that you should first save up on your Euro trip first—better be ready than sorry. You should also brush up on some foreign languages coz you can't expect everyone to speak English while you're there.

2. South America

Some places in South America are very interesting. If you're bringing someone along with you on your first vagabonding trip (maybe it will last about a few months for the first time) then find places that can be quite romantic. Some of the places that Potts recommends include Chile, Bolivia, Ecuador, Peru, among others. Always consider the language and if you speak Spanish or Portuguese then these may be really good options for you.

3. Southeast Asia

On the upside, visiting Southeast Asia will be cheap. In some of these places, if you bring $20,000 you end up with about a million in the local currency. But you don't have to bring that much cash with you.

Some of the pros in these destinations include ease of travel, friendliness of the locals, and also they're downright inexpensive. There are also a lot of exotic places in Asia, which makes them really interesting places to see.

You will have trouble though with the language. There are literally hundreds of languages even in one country alone. Potts' top pick was Thailand. But he also recommends other places like China, Burma, Indonesia, Malaysia, Vietnam, and Laos.

4. Middle East

The Middle East for the most part is also cheap. The locals here are also quite friendly. Potts recommends Egypt as a great starting point. You can then decide where to travel from there. He recommends Turkey, Lebanon, Jordan, and Syria as some of the best places.

And of course Israel is another amazing place especially if you also want to try a religious pilgrimage—if you are a religious type that is. Note that are places there that will require an Israeli stamp on your passport before you can enter the country—like Syria. Take note of these regulations before you start your journey.

5. Australia

Okay so Australia is definitely friendly to vagabonds and nomads alike. There are no language barriers here too—they speak English—hurrah! Well, you can also find work here too (and you should!) because Australia is rather expensive for vagabonding. From here he recommends that people go to the south pacific or even to New Zealand, which is also another great place.

How to Pick the Right Destination?

Of course those are Rolf Potts' top picks and that doesn't necessarily mean that they are the best picks for you. Remember that even though the points he made were truly valid, that is not a one size fits all kind of thing.

Your unique taste and needs will be different. Also, remember that the first time you go out on that big journey is always the hardest. It gets easier the next time around. So, making this first journey is the one that will either make it or break it for you.

The first time you will do this will require you to step out of your comfort zone. Sure you may have tried backpacking within the US but that is a totally different thing altogether. Culture shock may even become an issue for you if you begin traveling to exotic destinations.

Of course, there are a few factors that you need to consider when choosing the first place out of the country where you will go vagabonding. Let's go over them, shall we?

1. Try to Pick a Place Based on Your Passion/Hobby

Are you an artist or do you just adore art? Maybe you can tell which painting in a group is a Van Gogh? If art is your passion then maybe a vagabonding trip in any of the European centers of art will be a slice of heaven for you—France or England, take your pick. This is a big guarantee that you will be more than interested in the things that you will see and do there.

Are you into motor racing? Then maybe a trip to Singapore or Spain is in order since they are big in Formula 1 racing. Choose a place based on your passion and/or hobby. Are you a fan of Italian cuisine? Can you cook Italian food like a pro? Then go to Italy and see and taste genuine Italian for yourself. Basing your destination on your passion will make the trip a lot more worth it.

2. Choose Destinations That Have a Special Connection to You

If one of your parents is Asian then maybe a trip to Asia will be a good pick for you. Choose a place that has a personal connection to you. Maybe your grandparents were from that place.

If you have relatives there then you can live there near them or with them for a few months. That way staying in a foreign country won't feel so weird after all. That connection doesn't have to be family related. Maybe a good friend of yours moved there for some reason.

At least, when you travel and go vagabonding in that country you have someone you know who can show you around. If it is family then you can get free lodging for a time while you're still getting settled in and acclimating to the local culture. They can even show you around and teach you how things go in the country.

3. Always Consider the Language

Language barrier is a huge issue whenever you travel abroad for whatever reason. This is a major thing that you should consider when you travel abroad especially if you are vagabonding for the first time.

Don't expect the locals to know English fluently (or whatever your native language is). It will make your first trip a lot easier if you go to country where the locals speak your native language quite well.

Another alternative is that if you know another language, maybe you took some Spanish or you also spoke Spanish or some other language at home, then you should go to places that also spoke Spanish. That might mean considering South American destinations and other Spanish speaking countries.

Just don't let the language be a problem for your first trip. In your next vagabonding trips (after you have gained some experience), you can try your knack at learning a new language. It will be fun.

4. Travel Distance

How much time do you have available for your full-ofledged vagabonding experience. I recommend at least a month to about a few months first especially if you're going abroad to a different country. Take note of the legal requirements since some countries will only grant you a tourist visa and the length of your stay may be limited.

I don't recommend going out to some far-flung corner of the world for your first vagabonding trip. Take it from me—anything over 24 hours on a plane is absolutely exhausting. But if you're in Europe traveling by train then maybe you can make it an enjoyable ride as you try to get to know your fellow passengers.

Remember, if it is your first try at vagabonding overseas don't waste the experience by getting a really tiring trip. Keep things simple at first—it doesn't have to be a baptism of fire. Make it fun!

5. Go Easy on Your Budget

I recommend choosing a cheap destination first. That means London, Osaka (Japan), Sydney, Copenhagen (Denmark), Zurich, Tokyo (Japan), New York, Seoul (South Korea), Tel Aviv (Israel) and other expensive places are out.

Rule of thumb: you don't need to spend a ton of cash to make sure that your vagabonding trip is a great one. Make sure that your fund pools last as long as they can. If you can find a way to make them last 3 to 4 trips then that is another stellar achievement.

6. Pay Attention to the Season

The peak season is different for each part of the world. It may be really hot in June where you're from but it is already the storm season in some tropical paradise in some other part of the globe.

I would also suggest that for your first trip that you should avoid destinations that have very different climates that where you're from. You don't want to spoil your trip by getting sick because of the changes in the weather. You're in a vagabonding trip to see the world—not to see the four walls of their best hospitals (note that hospital services in some countries are outright terrible).

If you come from a warmer country (like Australia), then you may have some difficulty adjusting to extremely cold temperatures in other countries. So if you are planning a vagabonding trip to a country with really cold winters then start vagabonding in summer (their summer not yours). That way you can give yourself some time to adjust to the colder climate.

7. Book Ahead

Speaking of making your fund pools last, I also suggest that you plan ahead and book ahead. If you can book your trip to and from that country ahead of time then do so. Sure air fares fluctuate but you can never be sure if the prices will go down by the time you are ready to head back home.

You should also try to book your initial accommodations ahead of time. That would mean the hotel that you will stay in for a few days until you find some other place cheaper. Yes, you will have to find cheaper accommodations—and there are cheaper ones like houses for rent or even just a room for rent.

Some locals rent out parts of their homes to foreigners. A lot of times they're way cheaper than any hotel. Just check out the neighborhood and see if the condition of the room is to your liking coz that will be home for a few weeks or maybe months.

My Recommended List of Places to Visit – A Quick List

I have below my very own recommended places for vagabonds—especially for first timers. But I will have to warn you that I have included a list of places that are a tad too expensive.

I chose these places based on a few factors like the following:

- Night life
- English speaking folks (their ability to speak English)
- How friendly the locals are
- One way plane ticket price
- Air quality—you need to check the current AQI index for each city. It changes every now and then.
- How heavy the traffic is
- Safety ratings
- Internet speed
- Weather and overall temperature
- Cost of living
- Is it visa free or not
- Different city types

Now, without further ado, here is my list:

1. Best countries when it comes to internet speed, safety, weather, etc.

- Armenia
- Bosnia-Herzegovina
- Serbia
- Serbia
- Thailand
- South Korea
- Portugal
- Hungary
- Croatia
- Czech Republic

2. Best cities for first time vagabonds by air quality, friendliness, internet speed, etc.

- Budapest, Hungary
- Prague, Czech Republic
- Oaxaca, Mexico
- Florianopolis, Brazil
- Las Palmas, Spain
- Phuket, Thailand
- Taghazout, Morocco
- Bangkok, Thailand
- Kota Kinabalu, Malaysia
- Chiang Mai, Thailand

3. Countries with the lowest cost of living.

- India
- Philippines
- Nepal
- Morocco
- Pakistan
- Georgia
- Tunisia
- Indonesia
- Algeria
- Bangladesh
- Moldova
- Colombia
- Egypt
- Syria
- Macedonia

4. Countries that have the highest cost of living for nomads

- Switzerland
- Belgium
- Norway
- France
- Venezuela
- Ireland
- Iceland
- UK
- Denmark
- Finland
- Australia
- Luxembourg
- New Zealand
- Kuwait
- Singapore

Keep Things Simple

Don't plan a grand trip all over Europe or maybe country hopping in Asia. Well, at least not for your first trip. It can be exhausting and you may burn yourself out if you do. Take your time to enjoy the experience. It can be a bit difficult at times and there will be hassles along the way (trust me on that). Sometimes they treat you like a queen and there are times when they treat you like a cash cow or something.

Keep things small, keep things simple, and try to get an immersive experience. Let your first trip be something truly memorable.

And by the way, try not to judge the vagabonding lifestyle by this first trip. Your first vagabonding experience is your way of testing the waters. Not all trips will be the same and some will be a lot better than others.

Choose your destinations wisely using the tips mentioned here.

Chapter 9: It's Not a Vacation

Remember that vagabonding is not a vacation. As you should know by now, a vacation is care free (well, it should be), relaxing, enjoyable, and it is a frantic way to squeeze a year's worth of fun in two weeks or less.

Vagabonding on the other hand is something which is also fun and it can also be care free at times. It is also a relaxing experience and it is certainly something enjoyable. Yet it is also life as usual. You're not in a hurry to get things done—you're living life.

Adjusting to Life on the Road

One of the big differences between vagabonding and a vacation is that you need to adjust to life on the road. Vagabonding is a long term trip which means you need to make life on the road a lifestyle of your very own.

Someone who vagabonds never really returns home completely from the trip they made. You may come home of course to check out on your home (which you should have rented out for some added income stream), save money, visit with friends and family, and get your affairs in order.

However, the mindset is focused on life on the road. Your long-term goal is to go back on the road again. The ideal is to seek out new experiences instead of acquiring the latest in fashion, fads, and trends.

Adjusting to life on the road can be a bit of a challenge at first. The goal behind it is to go outside of your comfort zone. Yes, when you're out on the road in a new place on earth you will try out new things and experiences.

You're in a new place to live, work, and explore new things and the goal is to do that for a few years at a time. Taking on the challenge of going out of your comfort zone does have a few lasting benefits.

1. First off it makes you more open and accepting of other cultures and people.
2. It gives you a sense of wonder and curiosity – and if you satisfy that curiosity it will make you a better person.
3. It improves your overall street smarts. I must warn you that the world isn't a completely innocent and wonderful place full of unicorns and cute little ponies. There are unscrupulous people out there who will want to take advantage of you. It takes time to develop street smarts, which is why I

recommended that you take things slow. Take your vagabonding experience one step at a time.

Learning New Social Skills

Did I ever tell you that I am a natural introvert? I was really quite shy. I was the kind of person who would just sit down in the subway train and keep to myself until I get to my stop. I am usually the kind of person who would shy away from conversations and distance myself from parties. I'm the person on the sidelines just casually observing and minding my own business.

Now, imagine being out on a nomadic trip—you will have to learn how to talk to people. I soon realized during my first trip—it was just out of state—that being shy and utterly quiet wasn't going to cut it. I didn't know where I was. Sure I had Google maps but that can only go so far especially if you're in some far flung neck of the woods.

When you're lost, and this happened to me the first time I went vagabonding for a few weeks, you can't expect people to notice that you don't know where you're going. People just assume that you're on your way and you probably have an idea where it is you're supposed to be going to.

I also realized something—people will be generally kind enough to point you in the right direction if you ask politely. If you're out in a new country and you don't know where the nearest motel is you can't just stand on the side of the road and hope someone comes to you and tell you where it is—not everyone can mind read you know.

Bottom line is that you have to get some basic friendship skills.

That means you need to learn to open your mouth and start talking.

It starts with a simple greeting. I know that this is basic and you should have seen this done on Sesame Street or some other kid's show. If you're just asking for directions then there's no need to introduce yourself.

If it's just a casual conversation in a bar or a café somewhere then there is no need to introduce yourself as well—unless you want to of course. But then again introducing yourself by name opens people up and is a sign that you are friendly. People tend to respond to you better if you are at least willing to offer some personal info.

Tell them what you want, do some small talk, and share something about yourself. Make the convo pleasant.

The challenge here is that if you're abroad in another country the challenge is getting people to talk to you in your native language. Some will be happy to engage but a good number of them (in my experience this happens more in Asian countries) that people tend to shy away from the foreigner who speaks English.

They're just as shy as you are.

That is why one of my recommendations is to consider the spoken language in the place you chose to go to. If people have some good skills speaking in your native language or if you can talk in their language then you're in luck. You can strike up a conversation.

Mind your manners and be polite when you speak to the locals. Remember that even though you're living there for quite a while and you may even be employed by a local company you are still a guest. You live by their rules so be polite and avoid trouble. Just enjoy the local culture as you go.

Adjusting to the Local Cuisine

Traveling to a foreign country and literally moving there for a bit, i.e. not permanently, is both a challenge and an exciting adventure. It's a different environment and a totally different culture.

And in order to get immersed in a totally new culture is to sample the cuisine. The food in any country is an integral part of its culture. In fact, you can tell a lot about the people and the country's culture by the food they eat.

Here are a few tips to help you adjust to the local cuisine.

Tip #1—Don't Rush, Start Slowly

Take this bit of advice from me, the first time you arrive in a new location it will be stressful. It will be fun but all the adjustments that you have to make will definitely be a source of stress.

You will have to get settled in to your hotel. You can partially unpack your belongings. And then you have to get oriented to your surroundings. You have to know where work will be at—in case you were able to secure local employment.

You have to learn where the market is at, where the beach is at (and where all the other fun places are), where the local authorities are, where the shopping center is at, where the hospital or clinic is at, and other essential places are at.

You will also meet new friends. It is a tendency for people to gravitate towards the things that are familiar to them. That will happen to you too. You will want to stick to the familiar convenience stores that look like the little shops that you have back home. Those little fast food restaurants will make you feel like you're home.

You will eat the same kind of food that you used to it—and that happens a lot. However, you will have to learn how to try the local cuisine and eventually make it a part of you as well. After all, you will be living here in your new environment for a while.

That means you will have to extend your culinary comfort zone as it were. However, **don't just right in**. Some of the most exotic foods might shock you. Start off slowly and try new local dishes one bit at a time.

Of course your will make friends with the locals and they will at one point offer you some of their food. At times sharing their food is a sign of respect and hospitality.

Sometimes pushing the boundaries of the types of food that you can eat will become a necessity. One day you will come to a point when you can eat anything – well, almost anything.

Sure maybe you have tried some Japanese food, some Thai food, and maybe some Filipino food back home. But here's a secret—those restaurants back home, they only showcase a very small and limited version of the entire cuisine.

Let's take Japanese food for instance. Yeah, the sushi looks fun to eat even if it is raw meat. Teriyaki and other those fancy sounding food really looks great. But once you're in Japan you will be surprised to find out that there are a number of half wriggling strangely colored things that you have to put in your mouth.

The same thing is true in other countries. I have tried some scary looking bugs, worms, and insects in Thailand. Now, the balut egg is not the only dreaded thing that you will find in the islands of the Philippines. Wait until you get Soup #5 served to you. Google it if you want. There's even a Wikipedia page about it. Check out the pictures if you will but I don't recommend eating it.

In many countries when the locals serve you food it is their way of showing you their hospitality. In some cases they are offering you the best that they can give. And there will be instances especially when the family is really poor that they will offer you the only food that they ever have.

The polite thing to do is to at least sample the food. Take a bite and then tell them that it is delicious. You have to because in some cultures, like in Japan, if you refuse to eat the food they served the local folks will be greatly offended. Yep, do it even if you have to stomach something that is half alive in your mouth.

The rule of thumb here is to start slow but when people offer food and put it in front of you on the table make sure to eat. At least act like it's good. You don't have to hork it all in but at least eat something.

Now, here's something strange that totally goes against what I just told you. In some cultures, especially those who have been under Spanish colonial rule, it is customary to offer you the food they have on the table. But that is only a show of politeness to the guest.

If they offer you food to eat and they don't pull out a plate and a chair for you then you don't really have to eat. You just have to thank them for the offer. Just say thank you for the kind offer and then give an excuse like maybe you just ate and you're already full.

Case in point: learn the local customs when it comes to food. Don't rush to try every single piece of the local cuisine. Give your stomach and taste buds time to adjust to the new flavors and smells. Don't worry; you will adjust to it all in time.

Tip #2—Try Something New Each Day

To help you get up to speed with the local cuisine, challenge yourself to try something new every day. Just one thing should be enough. In fact, you can do it one restaurant or food shop at a time. Go to a new local store pick something on the menu or on the tray that you haven't tried before and eat it. After that, you're done. Oh yeah, you might want to bring a friend when you do this—at least you have some company to relish in the experience.

Tip #3—Don't Panic

Remember that if the locals eat it then you can be sure that it is edible. Well, that is even if you haven't considered them edible in the first place—imagine fried grass hoppers or sautéed snails. Yum!

Again, if they serve it to you, try one. At least one and then enjoy the flavors.

Tip #4—Take Your Time

Remember that the locals will be forgiving especially when they know that you are new in town. It will take time to develop a taste for the local cuisine and they will know that you are still getting settled. No rush. But make sure to apply some curiosity as you see new things and new food. Some of the people will be kind enough to warn you that some of their food may not be to your liking and when that happens it's okay not to try the questionable stuff on sale.

Making Cultural Adjustments

Living in a new culture that is quite different from your own is both exciting and challenging at the same time. You don't only have to deal with the new cuisine you will also have to learn new customs and behaviors as well.

Even if you have traveled around the world a lot, you will still find some forms of culture to be challenging albeit shocking at times. Remember that everyone goes through a period of cultural adjustment—everyone!

Hello Culture Shock

Social norms, traditions, and even values can get challenged when you're in a new culture. How you think things should be can be quite different in other places. Of course it is understandable that you carry with you your own culture—it's the one that you were accustomed to since you're so used to it since birth.

Culture shock is a very common experience when you go vagabonding. It involves feelings of confusion, disorientation, and also stress which happens when you experience new and different culture. Note however that people have varying reactions when they undergo cultural adjustments.

You can experience culture shock in varying degrees but in time there will only be a few things that would surprise you. Some of the symptoms or common reactions to new cultures include the following:

- Exhaustion
- Significant amounts of nervousness
- Becoming irritated over little things—especially some of the habits of the locals that are against your own culture
- Inability to concentrate
- Sleep difficulties
- Physical symptoms like aches and pains
- You may sometimes want to avoid social situations and get-togethers
- Extreme homesickness

Strategies That You Can Use When You Adjust to the Local Culture

Here are a few tips for handling culture shock. Remember that there will always be something that will strike you as being just way too weird. The reaction is common—you will wish that you were home.

1. Culture Shock is Normal and It Is Relative

Understand that it is all normal. Whatever reactions you are having everyone has had them one time or another. Another thing that you should realize is that everything is relative. Some may feel that your communication style is too direct, some may think that it is not direct enough, some people may perceive you to be too frank, and others may think that you are not assertive enough.

Remember that even in the local culture there are also subcultures and trying to adjust to every single detail will take time. You're not the only one adjusting to the locals, the locals are also adjusting to you. So, you're basically in the same boat. So don't make so much of a deal about it.

2. Create Your Own Space

Remember that I told you to learn how to travel light. That will come in handy since you don't know how big a space the local accommodations are. And that will also give you plenty of room to customize and tweak your room just the way you like it.

Make that little home space your refuge from all the crazy weird things that everyone is doing in your new environment. Hang a photo of home or bring out that thing which reminds you of who you are. Let your home or rented space be your sanctuary when you just can't take it anymore.

3. Be Open Minded and Curious

Be inquisitive. Be curious but not judgmental. Take with you that sense of wonder and awe. Ask questions. Try to learn something new about the place and the people. Take the advice from best-selling author Stephen Covey—seek first to understand before you seek to be understood.

Pay attention to non-verbal communication. Ask about it from the locals as well. For instance, in Japan whenever you ask something that is deemed too personal or the person being asked is just unwilling to answer your inquiry then don't be surprised if all you get is a smile. That is a non-verbal gesture that is telling you to please don't go into that detail.

4. Find At Least One Thing about the Local Culture that You Really Love

Not everything in the new culture you're experiencing is weird. There will be a few things that will resonate with you and your values. Hang on to that because in spite of the many strange things happening around you there are things that you find in common with your own culture. **BIG TIP:** Build on common beliefs.

5. Make Friends with Fellow Travelers, Nomads, and Vagabonds

The good news is that you're not alone. There will always be other foreigners there with you and they too share the same weird experiences. Make friends, do things together, and explore and have adventures.

Of course you will also find locals who are very congenial to foreigners and they will understand that you are already freaked out. They can even help you get out of uncomfortable situations. These folks are called your cultural allies. They're your go to people in case things get too weird.

Living Without the Usual Home Comforts

When you go vagabonding in a foreign country the power may be different. So bring a power adapter. On top of that you will also live in conditions that don't have the usual comforts you had back home. So, be your own adapter.

You may have to settle for some inconveniences like not having hot water. If that means you have to boil your own bathwater then do it. If it gets too hot you better ask around what the locals do to get cooler during warm weather—they may even suggest some nice place you can go to which is cooler and offer you some cool icy desserts. Ask around and the locals will be happy to answer your inquiries.

Chapter 10: Vagabonding with a Companion and The Mistakes You Should Avoid

Vagabonding alone by yourself is somewhat the norm. However, you can also bring someone with you—and hope that you don't end up killing each other along the way (pun intended).

Can Vagabonding Be A Couples Thing?

It might (big grin).

You see, I met a couple on the road and they did well but they had their issues. I guess living a nomadic life with someone will test you in different ways—in more ways than one actually.

Before you answer that question—and I'd leave it all up to you—here are some of the things that you will have to work with together.

Tolerate and Respect Other People's Culture and Beliefs

Some people are more judgmental about other beliefs and cultures. If you can work on that and agree on the terms on how to interact with the locals together then that will work quite well. The more you two are able to respect other people's differences the better it will be for the both of you.

How Well Can You Depend on Each Other in Times of Trouble?

Can you get in trouble with the local authorities while you're vagabonding? Yes, definitely—that's a possibility that you will have to plan for. Can you depend on each other during tough times? What if you're stuck in the middle of the road and you get a flat tire?

To make matters worse, it begins to rain cats and dogs. Now, what do you do? How you two react to these tough situations will tell how deep your relationship is and how well you can depend on each other.

How Well Can You Work Together?

Since you are traveling and vagabonding together it is only right to split tasks up. Each of you should be able to pitch in on the effort to keep the apartment clean, do the laundry, get shopping done, and shoulder part of the expenses as well.

Are You Willing to Make Adjustments?

Both of you should be willing to make adjustments—it's not just one party. Consider your style of travel if it matches that of your companion. If you are able to meet halfway and keep your commitments to one another then you're in good terms.

Vagabonding Mistakes to Avoid

Now, to help you along the way, here are some of the traveling mistakes that you should avoid. Of course you can also use these tips in case you are vagabonding by yourself.

- *Don't eat near major tourist spots*—the prices tend to double and the flavors are just the same.
- *Never exchange money at the airport*—exchange rates there are terrible.
- *Don't use travelers checks, in fact don't bring them*—they're useless nowadays.
- *Don't use your bank cards with fees*—the charges will kill you. At the very least use them sparingly.
- *Don't use US search engines*—Google has Google and whatever country you're in. Make sure to turn on the location service so when you search for places, you will easily find local hot spots.
- *Never skip travel insurance*—this is a lifesaver. Do it. Trust me.
- *Don't stay at hotels. Look for hostels, B&Bs, Pension Houses, and living spaces rented out by locals instead*—it's a great way to experience local culture and they're cheaper too. They're usually part of the local hospitality network. Ask other travelers, tourists, and other vagabonds/nomads you meet. They can nose you in the right direction.
- *Avoid local taxis*—find other means of transport. Taxis will rob you while you're awake—a lot of them will but there are honest taxi drivers, but don't take risks. If you meet a dependable one then take his number and contact him for future services.
- *Don't skip visiting the local tourism office*—they may have a few tips and info that can be useful even if you are staying there long term. You may even meet others who are vagabonding too so it would be a great place to find like-minded people.

- *Always carry spares of your most important gear*—that includes photocopies of your documents.

Vagabonding Equipment Checklist

The following is a checklist of the basic stuff that you will need on a long term trip. This list might come in handy to prepare you to avoid the usual hassles of nomadic life:

- Backpack/small luggage
- Wallet
- 1 formal attire/dress for formal occasions and serious stuff
- 1 pair of travel pants
- 1 pair of shorts for the beach and stuff
- 2 t-shirts (you can always buy this locally)
- Footwear
- Sunglasses
- Sunscreen
- Toiletries (minimal amount—you can just buy them on location)
- Medical supplies—especially antibiotics and other prescriptions. Make sure to bring enough to last you your entire trip because you can't always buy them in the country where you're going.
- Phone
- Power bank
- Laptop
- Universal power adapter
- Camera
- Car adapter with USB charging port
- Combination lock
- 1 multi-tool
- 1 dry bag

Conclusion: Adjusting to Life After Long Term Travel

Now, at one point in time you will come back home to see how things are doing. You will feel just as weird when you arrive home just like when you first arrived in foreign lands. The culture will be different—again.

Share Your Adventures

Your friends and family will love to hear your adventures. Remember that you should have gone digital which means your pictures and videos should have been cloud stored. Take the time to build new habits while you're home and look for new friends as well. You've learned how to socialize and make new friends abroad; it's time to put those same skills to use. It's a way to keep yourself sharp—vagabonding wise.

Take Time to be Finished with Your Trip

You will miss the people you met along the way. Cherish them. Post your experiences and their pictures on social media. I call this phase the grieving process. You can't always be sure to get back to them again sometime soon but you will have to learn how to move on. Besides, you can always plan other trips in the future.

Create a New Normal

You don't totally come back as you were. Once you have made traveling a habit this is your new normal. You're just not the same anymore. You learn to live simply, shut the TV, cook your favorite exotic meals, and all the other stuff you did while you were away. Don't try to switch off the vagabond that is in you.

Make Home a New Start

Treat home as a new phase in your vagabonding experience. You can't slip back into your old lifestyle. It just isn't you anymore. The only logical thing to do is to do what you have learned to do while you were away—personalize your home and treat it like that space you rented. Let this stage be another phase in your travels since you will be traveling again eventually.

Manage Your Expectations

You are not the only person that changed after your travels. The other people back home have changed and so apply the same openness and non-judgmental stance that you have used when you were away. It's a new skill that will come handy when you return home.

Prepare yourself to rebuild relationships. Prepare yourself also to make new friends.

Relax

You're home! Take time to relax and enjoy your own private space. You're back to the luxury of hot water, AC, and other modern stuff. But don't allow yourself to get pulled back by material things.

Relax and stay positive. Enjoy the moment while it lasts.

Decide

Finally, after making your first vagabonding trip it's time to decide whether this is a lifestyle that is just for you. You have sampled it and now you have to think if you want to keep it up or not.

The choice is yours and I don't blame you if you don't want to do it again. After all, vagabonding is not for everyone.

I hope that you enjoyed this book as much as I enjoyed putting in my thoughts and experiences in it. I hope this was able to help you get a bird's eye view of what it's like out there.

The next step of course is to decide if you want to do some long term travel and start making your plans today.

72718477R00038

Made in the
USA
Middletown, DE